JY - - '73

UNSOLVED MYSTERIES

The Escape from Alcatraz

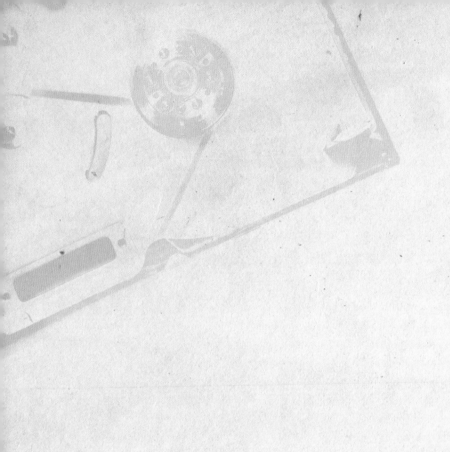

ABDO
Publishing Company

The Escape from Alcatraz

By Stephanie Watson

Content Consultant

Michael Esslinger
Historical researcher
and author

CREDITS

Published by ABDO Publishing Company, PO Box 398166, Minneapolis, MN 55439. Copyright © 2012 by Abdo Consulting Group, Inc. International copyrights reserved in all countries. No part of this book may be reproduced in any form without written permission from the publisher. The Essential Library™ is a trademark and logo of ABDO Publishing Company.

Printed in the United States of America,
North Mankato, Minnesota
122011
012012

 THIS BOOK CONTAINS AT LEAST 10% RECYCLED MATERIALS.

Editor: Melissa York
Copy Editor: Chelsey Whitcomb
Series design: Becky Daum, Christa Schneider, & Ellen Schofield
Cover production: Christa Schneider
Interior production: Becky Daum

Library of Congress Cataloging-in-Publication Data
Watson, Stephanie, 1969-
   The escape from Alcatraz / by Stephanie Watson.
      p. cm. -- (Unsolved mysteries)
   Includes bibliographical references.
   ISBN 978-1-61783-303-8
   1. United States Penitentiary, Alcatraz Island, California--Juvenile literature. 2. Escapes--California--Alcatraz Island--Case studies--Juvenile literature. 3. Escaped prisoners--California--Alcatraz Island--Case studies--Juvenile literature. I. Title.
   HV9474.A4W38 2012
   365'.641--dc23
                                        2011039553

Table of Contents

Chapter 1

Escape from the Rock

It was shortly after 9:30 p.m. on the night of June 11, 1962. The 22-acre (9-ha) island of Alcatraz was shrouded in darkness and fog. Atop the battleship-shaped hunk of sandstone rock, the cell house was also in darkness.

ALCATRAZ ISLAND: Alcatraz stretches approximately 1,075 feet (32.8 m) across and 850 feet (25.9 m) wide. Its top peak reaches approximately 130 feet (40 m) above sea level.

The wind—which was so icy that it felt more like January than June—screeched through the barred windows. Every few seconds, fog horns bleated their mournful tone throughout the cell house, where approximately 250 of the country's toughest prisoners lay in hard, narrow cots. The final check of the night and lights-out were past. Now the men had nothing to do but sleep or lie awake and contemplate their dismal futures—the hours upon hours that still stretched ahead of them in the super-maximum security prison nicknamed the Rock.

Three of the prisoners at Alcatraz were not sleeping, however. They also were not thinking about

Alcatraz is located in the middle of San Francisco Bay in California.

A World Away

Alcatraz is only 1.25 miles (2 km) from the shores of San Francisco, California, yet it might as well have been a world away for the prisoners who lived there. In fact, Alcatraz is about as barren and desolate as an island located that close to civilization can be.

Although Alcatraz is an island, there is no real beach. Before people developed the island, there was no sand, soil, or plant life. There is no source of freshwater; what is not collected from rain and fog has to be brought across the bay by boat.

their future on the island. Instead, they were thinking about freedom— the freedom that, after so many years behind bars, was now achingly close. At that moment, these three career criminals—Frank Lee Morris and brothers John and Clarence Anglin—were setting off into the frigid waters of San Francisco Bay. They were about to escape from Alcatraz.

It was a plot that had been more than a year in the making. Morris and the Anglins had managed to steal enough supplies to handcraft the raft on which they made their escape. The men had assembled a whole collection of handmade accessories, which included life vests, drills, a flashlight, and a periscope. They had sculpted such realistic models of their own heads that not a single prison guard realized that dummies, and not the men themselves, were occupying their beds.

Over the past year, the three men (plus at least one other accomplice) had tunneled through the solid concrete walls of their cells and set up their very own workshop at the top of the cell house, all without raising any suspicion. They had evaded steel bars, gun galleries, and manned watchtowers.

Earlier on this same night, Morris and the Anglins had escaped through the cell house roof, slid 50 feet (15 m) down a pipe to the ground, scaled two barbed wire-topped fences, and run down two embankments without alerting any of the guards on duty. They were about to set in motion one of the most brazen and best-planned prison escape attempts ever to be undertaken in the US prison system. Their escape would become renowned as one of the greatest unsolved mysteries of all time, and it would launch one of the biggest manhunts in history—a manhunt that still continues today.

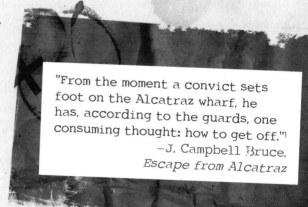

"From the moment a convict sets foot on the Alcatraz wharf, he has, according to the guards, one consuming thought: how to get off."[1]
—J. Campbell Bruce,
Escape from Alcatraz

By the time the three men had set off into San Francisco Bay, they had joined a long legacy of convicts who had tried to escape from Alcatraz. Some of the hopeful escapees had been shot and killed during their attempt. A few drowned in the murky, frigid San Francisco Bay waters. Others were found shivering in those waters and returned in handcuffs to their cells. At least one man found the water so cold and inhospitable that he came crawling back to Alcatraz. Of all these escape attempts, the

Roof of the Alcatraz cell house

one orchestrated by Morris and the Anglins was by far the most sophisticated.

Did the three escapees make it? It is a question that historians and investigators are still struggling to answer. Although there has been a lot of speculation and many supposed sightings, no one can say for sure what became of Frank Morris and John and Clarence Anglin. Whatever their fate, the three men showed every prison engineer, designer, and warden that Alcatraz was not the escape-proof fortress it was constructed to be. It might have been difficult to escape from Alcatraz, but it certainly was not impossible.

Chapter 2

The History of Alcatraz

What must people have thought when they first set eyes on this desolate outcropping of rock? Native Americans were probably the first to take rafts to the island that would eventually become known as Alcatraz, but there is no evidence they lived there.

In 1775, Spanish naval lieutenant Don Juan Manuel de Ayala spotted the mass of rock jutting from the water. Because the island was covered with white pelicans, he named it after them— La Isla de los Alcatraces, or The Island of the Pelicans. Later, the island's name was shortened and Americanized to Alcatraz.

By the mid-1800s, Alcatraz, as well as the rest of the state of California, was part of Mexico. After the Mexican-American War of 1846–1848, America took control of the state, and with it, Alcatraz.

A Fortress

The US government worried that foreign invaders might also take an interest in California. To protect San Francisco Bay, the government planned to build a series of fortresses. With $500,000 in funding from Congress, construction of the Alcatraz fortress began in the winter of 1853.

The fortress was built to withstand even the most vigorous attack. Thick walls surrounded it, and huge cannons guarded it from all sides. A three-story brick citadel atop the island housed military officers.

In the middle of the nineteenth century, the

Alcatraz's Arsenal

When the Alcatraz fortress was completed, it was a formidable sight. Protected by more than one-half mile (0.8 km) of brick, granite, and sandstone walls 30 feet (9 m) tall, the fortress was armed with an arsenal threatening enough to make any would-be invaders pause. Lining its perimeter were more than 100 cannons with enough power and range to sink approaching ships three miles (5 km) out at sea.

Yet even with all of that firepower, the cannons were never shot in a real battle. Eventually, the weapons became obsolete and the government stopped using Alcatraz as a military fortress.

government began to realize the island's unique potential as a military prison. Its remote location made it an ideal place to house prisoners. During the American Civil War (1861–1865) and Spanish-American War (1898), the government sent Confederate sympathizers and military offenders to Alcatraz. This would mark the beginning of Alcatraz's long history as a prison. In time, it would also house spies, foreign combatants, and some of the most wanted criminals in the United States.

As the number of prisoners at Alcatraz grew, additional buildings were constructed in which to house them. By 1904, the prison could accommodate more than 300 men. Three years

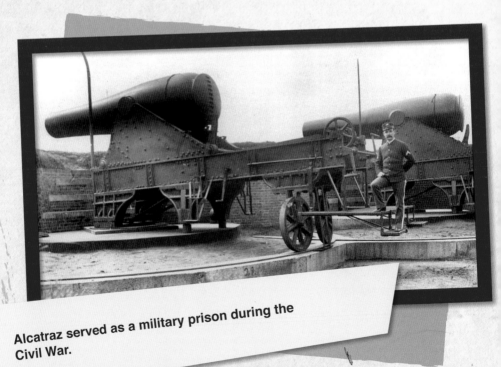

Alcatraz served as a military prison during the Civil War.

later, Alcatraz was officially designated as the Pacific Branch of the United States Military Prison.

Alcatraz was not yet the tough superprison it would eventually become. There were few guards, and the cells were barely secure. Taking advantage of the lax security, some prisoners tried to escape. Although no one stopped them, most grew chilled swimming in the cold water and either drowned or returned to Alcatraz.

A New Superprison

Alcatraz remained a military prison for more than 80 years, until 1933. Then another need arose. A new breed of criminal was on the prowl, and the US government needed new ways to lock up lawbreakers.

In the 1920s and 1930s, America's greatest public enemies operated in the shadowy underworld

Alcatraz Expands

By the turn of the twentieth century, the population of Alcatraz was expanding. To avoid overcrowding, new prison cells were needed to house the extra prisoners.

The old fortress was torn down and a new cell house was constructed using the island's own labor source— prisoners. The new cell house was quite a feat of engineering. At the time, it was the largest steel-reinforced concrete structure in existence. It was large enough to hold hundreds of inmates, as well as a hospital, kitchen, mess hall, library, and shower rooms.

of gambling, bank robbery, and liquor bootlegging. Men including Al Capone, George "Machine Gun" Kelly, and John Dillinger had set off a large crime wave.

Coincidentally at this same time, the US military realized it was too expensive to house military prisoners on an island where every supply had to be brought in by boat. When the War Department abandoned Alcatraz as a prison, the Department of Justice took over the property.

To show that it was serious about stopping crime, the government turned Alcatraz into a superprison to hold the most notorious and dangerous criminals. It would serve as a warning to anyone who

The Making of a Maximum Security Prison

When Alcatraz was turned into a federal prison in 1934, security expert Robert Burge was put in charge of making it escape-proof. This would not be an easy task, considering that the original prison had such minimal security. Burge had a budget of $260,000 and the latest technology at his disposal.

He set to work replacing the flimsy materials of the original cells and windows with tool-proof steel bars. He installed chain-link fencing topped with barbed wire around the perimeter of the prison. A new locking system was installed that allowed the guards to open one cell or a whole row of cells at once. Metal detectors were installed at the entrance of the dining hall, the recreation yard, and the prison industries where the prisoners would work once they arrived. No longer would it be easy to escape from Alcatraz.

dared threaten the American way of life that they would not get away with it and they would never escape. Alcatraz was officially turned into a federal prison on January 1, 1934. The new superprison would operate under the watchful eye of Warden James A. Johnston.

On August 11, 1934, the first group of prisoners arrived at Alcatraz from the federal penitentiary in Atlanta, Georgia. They were followed a few weeks later by another set of prisoners from Leavenworth

Warden Johnston points out the prison's top-of-the-line security system after a 1946 escape attempt.

Penitentiary in Kansas. By the end of the year, 200 prisoners called Alcatraz home.

Extra care had to be taken when transporting such dangerous criminals. The prisoners were herded onto trains. Chained and handcuffed in their train cars, they traveled across the country guarded by an officer in a wire cage with a loaded shotgun. Once the trains reached the shores of San Francisco Bay, they were loaded onto a railroad barge and towed across the bay while being carefully watched by the US Coast Guard.

NO HOPE: A reporter who was at Alcatraz when the first prisoners arrived wrote, "It was made clear that the prisoners, the most vicious and desperate in the country, will not escape from Alcatraz."[2]

Once at Alcatraz, the men were led up a winding road. They shuffled along in manacles, their feet bare or covered only by thin slippers. Warden Johnston said the men arrived "hot, dirty, weary, unshaved, depressed, desperate, showing plainly that they felt they were at the end of the trail."[1] The men were led in pairs to the main cell house. There, they were photographed, stripped, and given numbers. A doctor checked them over before they were told to march, naked, to their new cells with their clothes in their hands.

As the prisoners took that first long march to their cells, they had no idea what their future would bring. They probably hoped for release, and some were lucky enough to see that hope realized. Others left in straightjackets, driven insane by the endless, mind-numbing prison routines. A few men tried to escape. Most escapees drowned, were shot and killed, or returned to their cells to wait out the rest of their jail time. Less than a handful of prisoners disappeared off the island, never to be seen again.

Notorious Prisoners

Famous inmate Al Capone arrived at Alcatraz in an armored ferry on August 22, 1934. Some of America's most notorious gangsters were housed there over the years, including Arthur "Doc" Barker, George "Machine Gun" Kelly, Roy Gardner, and Floyd Hamilton.

Chapter 3

Life on the Rock

The Alcatraz cell house contained four blocks—A, B, C, and D. In the early years of Alcatraz's history as a prison, the A block was used for storage and occasionally for solitary confinement. In 1941, the D block became the only solitary confinement unit. At the time when Morris and the Anglins were held in Alcatraz, prisoners lived in the B and C blocks. Each block was made up of two banks with three tiers each. Each tier contained 28 cells, for a total of 336 cells. Behind the cells was a narrow corridor filled with sewer, water, and electric pipes.

Every area of Alcatraz had a special name and purpose. The corridor that ran between the B and

The corridor between B and C, also known as Broadway

C blocks was called Broadway. Prisoners who were unlucky enough to live along Broadway enjoyed little privacy because it was such a high-traffic area. At one end of Broadway was the main prison entrance. At the other end was the dining room. The area at the back of the cell house was called Times Square because of the big clock that hung there. The area in the C block that faced the library was called Park Avenue. Though it was not anywhere near as fancy as its namesake in New York, Park Avenue was considered the best real estate in the prison because the cells were warm compared to cells in the B block, and the inmates had at least some privacy.

Unlike most prisons at the time, Alcatraz gave prisoners their own cells.

The absolute worst place to live was in the D block—the isolation area that was known as the treatment unit (or just TU) to the guards and solitary or the hole to the prisoners. The D block contained 42 cells. Men who wound up in solitary had done something to get themselves into trouble. As a result, they were forced to sit in the hole for 24 hours a day. They even ate in their cells. The best cells in solitary looked much like the regular cells on Alcatraz. Five cells contained just a sink and toilet and were lit by a dim lightbulb. Worst of all was a pitch-dark cell called The Oriental, which had only a hole in the floor for its bathroom.

An inmate entering his cell for the first time might have been dismayed by its size. Cells measured only nine feet (3 m) long, five feet (2 m) wide, and seven feet (2 m) tall—approximately the size of a closet. Along the side of the cell was a narrow cot with a thin mattress. Across from the bed sat a small worktable. Along the back wall of the cell was a toilet. There was no privacy, and because the toilets flushed with salt water piped in from the bay, they always smelled terrible. Next to the toilet, attached to the wall, was a sink that ran cold water. Hot water faucets were not installed in cells until the early 1960s. Above the sink were two shelves where prisoners could store their few belongings. Below the shelves, wooden pegs provided a place for the men to hang their clothes, which consisted of gray pants and

The Oriental

For an Alcatraz inmate, the worst possible place to wind up was The Oriental. It was also called the Strip Cell—or, more commonly "the hole." It was where the inmates went for committing the most severe violations of prison rules.

When the door closed, prisoners were left in complete darkness. There was no toilet or sink—only a hole in the floor to use. For the entire day, inmates sat on the hard floor in the complete blackness, with no idea what time it was. At 9:30 p.m. they were given a mattress on which to sleep. Prisoners could spend days in this utter isolation.

shirt, cotton long underwear, socks, and a large blue handkerchief.

Along the base of the back wall was a metal ventilator grill. It measured only six by nine inches (15 by 23 cm) and was tightly welded to the concrete wall. As tiny and secure as it was, this grill would prove an essential part of the escape plan hatched by Morris and the Anglins.

Sleep, Eat, Work

Life was predictable on the Rock. Warden Johnston established the daily schedules in 1934, and they did not change much during the entire time the prison was open. The day started with a shriek of the 6:30 a.m. morning alarm, and from there it ran according to a strict schedule. Put on the prison-issued shirt, pants, and shoes. Stand at the bars for a head count. March in line to breakfast. Eat, work, eat, work, eat, and return in line to cell. In between these activities were at least 12 head counts. Lights out was at 9:30 p.m. sharp. Every day was like the one before it and the one after it. It was enough to drive some of the men mad enough to commit suicide. As former convict Brian Conway put it, "Men go slowly insane under the exquisite torture of routine."[1]

Twice a week the men took showers in the community shower room, which was located in the basement. Three times a week, the men were required to shave. No facial hair was allowed. Guards would pass out razors and then collect the blades as soon as the men had finished. Anyone who refused to shave was forcibly shaved by a guard and put in solitary.

Rules on the Rock

Warden Johnston also set up a strict set of rules for the prisoners. When they arrived at Alcatraz, the men were given a book outlining those rules. Everything from their clothing to how they set up their cell to how they ate was strictly controlled. Men had to keep their shoes under the bed, toilet paper on the ledge in front of the vent, and soap on the left side of the sink. In the mess hall, those who did not finish

A Prisoner's Day

This is the schedule prisoners at Alcatraz followed each day:

6:30 a.m. Wake up, make beds, clean up cells, wash, and dress

7:00 a.m. Walk in line to mess hall for breakfast

7:20 a.m. Work detail

9:30 a.m. Eight-minute rest, return to work

11:40 a.m. Mess hall for lunch

12:20 p.m. Return to work

2:30 p.m. Rest period

4:25 p.m. Mess hall for dinner

4:45 p.m. Return to cell

9:30 p.m. Lights out

Work was a privilege, and prisoners not allowed to work spent those hours alone in their cells.

25

Capone in his Cage

Al "Scarface" Capone was one of the most notorious gangsters of the Prohibition era. He made millions of dollars and was behind the infamous Saint Valentine's Day Massacre on February 14, 1929, in which seven men from a rival Chicago, Illinois, gang were murdered. Capone was never convicted of murder. He was sent to prison for tax evasion in 1932. He began his sentence in a federal prison in Atlanta, but it was too easy for him to bribe the guards and receive gifts from friends there. He was sent to Alcatraz in 1934 to isolate him from his gang. While in prison, he began to show signs of dementia. For a time, Warden Johnston had him confined to a bed surrounded by a metal screen. Inmates at the time called it the "bug cage." He was transferred to a mainland prison in 1939 and released later the same year. He lived quietly and privately until his death in 1947.

everything on their plate could spend more than a week in solitary subsisting on a diet of nothing but bread and water.

One of Warden Johnston's toughest rules was the code of silence. In the early years of Alcatraz, prisoners were not allowed to speak to each other in their cells, walking in line, or during head counts. The only times they could talk were while they were eating and while they were working, and even then they had to be quiet about it. Inmates who broke the code of silence also found themselves in solitary.

Small Comforts

SHOWER WATER: Just in case the prisoners had any ideas about trying to swim for shore, the shower water was kept warm. That way, inmates could not get used to cold water.

The men who were incarcerated at Alcatraz had no rights. They were there for one reason only—to serve time for the crimes they had committed. At Alcatraz, they were given a roof over their heads, food, basic clothing, and medical care. Everything else, from visitors to work, was a privilege they had to earn.

During their first three months at Alcatraz, prisoners were allowed no visitors. With good behavior, they could earn two visits a month. During those visits, prisoners spoke to friends and family through a small intercom in a window made of bulletproof glass. If the men broke the rules during those visits—meaning they mentioned anything about prison life or current events—they were cut off from further visitors.

Work might not sound like much of a privilege, but it was either that or sit in a tiny cell for an extra nine hours a day. The men could work in one of the prison's industries, which included a glove factory, rubber mat shop, clothing factory, prison laundry, and brush shop. There they stayed busy, learned skills they could take with them if they were ever released, and earned five to twelve cents an hour, the equivalent of approximately eighty cents to two dollars an hour today.

Inmates could fill the remaining hours of their day with a limited set of activities. Men who could afford musical instruments, such as a saxophone or accordion, could play them in the early evening—a time that became known as "Happy Hour." The men were also allowed to purchase art supplies such as paintbrushes, paint, and canvases from the prison. While some prisoners painted, others wrote letters or did crossword puzzles. One of the main sources of entertainment was the prison library, which housed thousands of books. Prisoners requested books from a catalog, and an inmate brought these books around to the prisoners' cells. Even though the books were censored, with all mentions of violence and crime removed, they allowed the prisoners' imaginations to transport them outside of the grim Alcatraz prison walls.

Inmates at work in the tailor shop, late 1930s

On the weekends, prisoners who behaved themselves were given a treat—a visit to the prison's recreation yard. Although it was surrounded by 20-foot- (6-m-) tall walls and a catwalk manned by armed guards, the yard offered prisoners a brief respite from the maddening routine inside. They could play bridge, handball, softball, or shuffleboard. On a clear day, they could gaze in envy at San Francisco landmarks, including the Golden Gate Bridge and Coit Tower. They may not have realized that on the other side of the bay, people were also looking at them. Tourists and residents used to line up along the San Francisco shore and put coins in high-powered telescopes to gape at the men incarcerated on Alcatraz.

Chapter 4

Security on Alcatraz

Alcatraz once housed some of the nation's most violent criminals. Others were not necessarily violent—they were in there for robbery or bootlegging—but they were sent to Alcatraz because they had tried to escape from other prisons. To prevent them from attempting another escape, security on the island had to be tough.

When Warden Johnston decided to make Alcatraz escape-proof, he

NO PRISON WILL HOLD ME: When Harvey Bailey got life in prison for kidnapping millionaire Charles Urschel in 1933, he famously said, "No prison will ever hold me." Alcatraz did hold him— for 12 years.

used every tool at his disposal. He installed the most sophisticated equipment available at the time. That included tool-proof steel bars, gun galleries and gun walks, gates with electric locks, metal detectors, and tear gas canisters.

The tight security began as soon as the boat carrying a load of convicts pulled up to the island's dock. To prevent any of the men from trying to hijack the boat and make their way back to the mainland, the skipper would attach the boat key to a line and send it up to a guard. That key would be returned to the skipper only when all of the island's convicts had been counted.

From there, the men were taken on foot or by bus up a narrow, twisty road. They shuffled along

Secure Cells

To foil any prisoners' attempts at sawing or filing through their cells, tool-proof bars were installed in all of the cells, as well as on all of the windows the prisoners could reach. The outside layer of these bars was made of soft steel, but inside was a core of hard steel that was virtually impossible to break through. The back wall of the cells was made of solid concrete, which was supposed to be impenetrable.

The guards could open and close the cells remotely using levers in control boxes on either side of the cell block. If they needed to, guards could open groups of as many as 15 cells at a time—such as in the morning when the men went to breakfast. They could also open one cell at a time.

Model Industries Building

Water Tower

Power House

Industries Building

Recreation Yard

Main Cell House

Boat Dock

Parade Grounds

Building 64 Residential Apartments

The buildings of Alcatraz

in handcuffs and leg irons. During the entire trip, a guard in a high tower kept a careful watch.

Inside the prison, a doctor gave each man a thorough and humiliating inspection. He looked inside their ears, nose, mouth, and rectum for any tools or other contraband items they might have brought in with them.

The Armorer

Though prisoners rarely entered or exited through the front of the prison, the area was highly secure. Anyone coming into or going out of the prison had to pass through three barred doors. These were not just any doors—they were made of solid steel and guarded by a man inside a bulletproof glass-enclosed control center. This guard was known as the armorer.

After visitors or prison officers came in through the main entrance, they went through a barred locked gate and found themselves inside an enclosed chamber with another locked gate on the other end. Shields covered the locks on the gates leading into and out of the chamber. The armorer was the only person who could open those shields.

The armorer would look through mirrors to see inside the chamber. If he noticed a prisoner alone in the chamber, he could lock the doors on either side of the chamber, trapping the person inside.

Prison guard demonstrating the cell-locking device, 1960

If everything looked clear, he would press a button to release the shield on the second steel door and allow the main gate officer to open the door and bring the person into or out of the main cell house. The doors were relocked as soon as the person stepped through them.

Every day, the armorer was given the head count at least a dozen times. If the count was off by just one prisoner, the armorer would immediately call the Coast Guard and San Francisco Police. If a riot broke out inside the prison, the armorer would hit the siren to alert all off-duty personnel. Then he would distribute an arsenal of rifles, machine guns, and grenades to the guards.

Watching Every Move

Prisoners could not do anything at Alcatraz without being watched. The guards who patrolled both inside and outside of the cell house made sure of that.

Around the entire perimeter of the cell block were heavy wire mesh-enclosed catwalks called gun galleries.

Alcatraz guards were among the toughest of their breed—smart and highly trained. Many were former soldiers or police officers. Unlike most prisons, which had an approximately 10-to-1 prisoner-to-guard ratio, the ratio at Alcatraz was one guard to every three inmates.

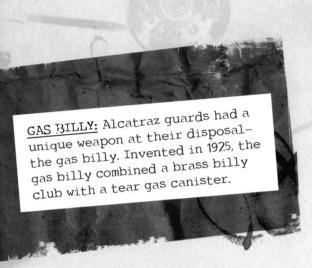

GAS BILLY: Alcatraz guards had a unique weapon at their disposal— the gas billy. Invented in 1925, the gas billy combined a brass billy club with a tear gas canister.

Guards patrolled these gun galleries all day and all night.

Watchtowers armed by officers with high-powered rifles oversaw the outside of the prison. They watched as the inmates walked to and from the shops and dock area. A guard in a tower at the north end of the dock looked out for any boats that drifted too close to the island or any prisoners who tried to slip into the water. Another tower on the roof of the Model Industries Building was staffed during the day when the men were at work. There was also a tower between the prison yard and industries, as well as a road tower. A main guard tower once watched over the roof of the cell house, but due to budget constraints it was removed in 1951. Had it still been there on that June evening in 1962, the guard inside would have surely seen the three men trying to make their escape.

Even when the prisoners were not being watched by live guards, their movements were still monitored.

Metal detectors located at the dock, outside the dining hall, in the prison entrance, and on the paths leading to and from the shops where the men worked made sure no one stole a fork, a saw, or any other item that could be used to break through bars or walls. Prisoners referred to these metal detectors as "mechanical stool pigeons."[2] A stool pigeon is a tattle-tale or an informer.

The Gas Chamber

The ceiling of the mess hall was speckled with small silver objects. Although they looked festive, like ornaments, they were actually tear gas canisters such as the one shown here. If a riot or fight broke out in the mess hall, guards in the gun gallery and outside towers could remotely trigger these canisters, releasing a cloud of choking fumes. This is how the convicts got their nickname for the mess hall. They called it the Gas Chamber.

Chapter 5

Escape Attempts

Despite the tool-proof bars and reinforced steel doors, the gun galleries and guard towers, and the frigid, turbulent waters surrounding Alcatraz, many men tried to escape. During the 29 years in which Alcatraz was a federal prison, 14 escape attempts were made involving 36 men. Twenty-three of the men were caught. Eight were either killed or drowned. Five were never seen again.

Joseph Bowers

Almost from the moment Alcatraz was transformed into a maximum security prison, the men who were incarcerated there talked about

Watchtowers guarded the prison, including one on the Industries Building.

and plotted their escape. One of the first prisoners to attempt it was Joseph Bowers.

While working outside the prison in August 1936, Bowers suddenly headed for the chain-link fence and started climbing. A guard shouted for him to get down. Bowers ignored him. The guard fired off two warning shots.

As Bowers reached the top of the fence and began climbing over the side, the guard shot again, this time hitting his target. Bowers dropped onto the rocks below, dead.

Ralph Roe and Theodore Cole

Oklahomans Ralph Roe and Theodore Cole had long criminal careers behind them by the time they found themselves on the same train bound for Alcatraz. Both men had committed their first robberies when they were just teenagers, and followed them up with a string of other crimes.

The two men also had something else in common. At different times, they both had tried to escape from McAlester Prison in Oklahoma—Roe in a utility crate and Cole in a laundry bag. Neither was successful. Roe ended up with a 99-year sentence at Alcatraz. Cole got 50 years. When Cole arrived he

Theodore Cole's mug shot

allegedly said, "Don't think I'll like it here. Doubt I'll stay long."[1]

Roe and Cole got to know each other while working in the mat shop, turning used car tires into rubber ship-deck mats for the US Navy. Over several weeks, they began to construct a plan. Slowly but deliberately, they started filing through two iron bars in a window of the mat shop using a stolen hacksaw.

On December 16, 1937, just before 1:00 p.m., the guard stepped away from the mat shop. Roe and Cole pried the loosened window bars open, broke the glass, and jumped out. They smashed through the lock on the gate leading down to the water. Using five-gallon (19-L) fuel canisters as floats, they slipped into the fog-shrouded water.

At the 1:30 p.m. head count, the guard realized the two men were missing. The armorer was notified. The Coast Guard, local police, and federal law enforcement officers searched the island and its surrounding waters for weeks. There was no sign of the two men.

What happened to Ralph Roe and Theodore Cole? Given how fast the currents were that day, most experts believe they were swept out to sea and died. Although a few people claimed to have seen

Swimming from Alcatraz: Possible or Impossible?

Could Ralph Roe and Theodore Cole have made it to shore in waters so cold and currents so strong? That is a matter of some debate.

Lloyd C. Whaley, a San Francisco city engineer, did not think so. "Small boats could not have bucked that current. A strong swimmer starting at Alcatraz would have found himself going out the Gate in the fog before he had expended sufficient energy to reach shore in still water," he said at the time.[2]

The current did not seem to bother seven-year-old Braxton Bilbrey, a second grader from Glendale, Arizona, who on May 22, 2006, swam the 1.4-mile (2.3-km) stretch from Alcatraz to San Francisco in just 47 minutes. A few months before, a nine year old had made the same swim in less than two hours. If two elementary school students could make the swim, was it possible that two full-grown convicts might have done the same?

On the other hand, the children had the advantage of wet suits and intense training. The prisoners got little exercise and would have had no opportunity to practice swimming. Even with the strength of full-grown men, escapees were at a considerable disadvantage.

the two men after their escape, no report was ever confirmed.

The First Violent Escape Attempt

The first few people who tried to escape from Alcatraz were sneaky, but none of them tried to harm the guards to make their getaway. That changed on May 23, 1938, with the escape attempt of James C. Lucas, Rufus Franklin, and Thomas R. Limerick.

Lucas had tried to murder

gangster Al Capone in prison with a pair of prison laundry shears. Franklin had been a thief since age 13. And, Limerick was considered the "No. 1 bank robber of the Northwest."[3]

Shortly after 2:00 p.m. on the afternoon of May 23, the three men decided to make their getaway from the woodworking shop. To escape, they first had to deal with guard Royal Cline. The men attacked, cracking Cline's skull with a hammer. Then they went out a window and climbed to the roof of the shop building, where gun tower guard Harold

James Lucas, *far left*, and Rufus Franklin, *second from left*, both received life sentences for killing a guard during their 1938 escape attempt.

Stites was keeping watch. Lucas, Franklin, and Limerick began throwing hammers, wrenches, and metal weights at the guard. Stites fired back at the men with his gun, hitting Limerick in the head and Franklin in both shoulders. Lucas hid behind a wall.

When it was all over, 36-year-old guard Royal Cline was dead. Limerick also died from his wound. Lucas and Franklin got life sentences for Cline's murder. Lucas later said, "It was a crazy scheme and I now realize how nutty we were."[4]

The Fourth Attempt

In Missouri in the 1920s and 1930s, Arizona "Ma" Barker took care of a gang of outlaws who became renowned for their kidnappings, robberies, and other crimes. One of her children, Arthur "Doc" Barker, landed in Alcatraz in 1935 for kidnapping wealthy banker Edward G. Bremer.

Arthur "Doc" Barker spent time in jail in Saint Paul, Minnesota, for the Bremer kidnapping before his transfer to Alcatraz.

Four years later, he was working on busting out.

Barker began planning his escape in 1938. He assaulted inmate Ira Earl Blackwood in the recreation yard to get himself thrown in

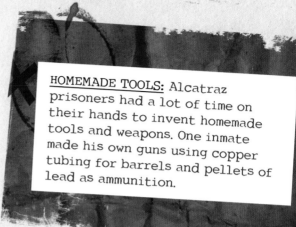

HOMEMADE TOOLS: Alcatraz prisoners had a lot of time on their hands to invent homemade tools and weapons. One inmate made his own guns using copper tubing for barrels and pellets of lead as ammunition.

solitary. It might sound strange that a guy who was trying to escape would want to go to solitary, but Barker knew the bars in the D block were older than those in the A and B blocks. They were made from softer metal—the type a hacksaw or other sharp tool could cut all the way through.

For days, Barker, Dale Stamphill, William "Ty" Martin, Henry Young, and Rufus McCain worked their cell bars. Once they were able to get out of their cells, they started working on the window bars. Each day, they would put all of the bars back in place with putty and cement so the guards would not spot anything unusual.

On Friday, January 13, 1939, the five men were ready to go. As soon as the guard had finished patrolling the D block, the men left their cells,

Crawling Back to Alcatraz

Floyd G. Hamilton was once at the top of the FBI's Most Wanted list. In April 1943, after a failed escape attempt, Hamilton hid out in one of the island's caves for two days. Finally, hungry and cold, he clawed his way back up the cliff, crawled into the same window through which he had escaped, and returned to prison.

climbed out the window, and dropped eight feet (2 m) to the path below. Once at the water's edge, they began tying pieces of wood together with their clothing to form a makeshift raft.

It did not take long for the guards to notice the men were missing and sound the alarm. Catching sight of the guards, the five escapees jumped into the water. The guards opened fire. Barker was killed. The other four men were returned to their cells.

After the attempt, everyone wanted to know what went wrong. How did these five men get so close to escaping? Federal Bureau of Prisons Director James V. Bennett vowed he would strengthen Alcatraz's defenses. He updated the D block with tool-proof bars and electronically controlled locks.

The Battle of Alcatraz

After the first four escape attempts, five more followed by the spring of 1946. With Roe and Cole missing and presumed dead, no one had succeeded.

One prison guard and several prisoners had died. The most violent breakout, the Battle of Alcatraz, was yet to come.

The plot started with Kentucky bank robber Bernard Paul Coy. His job was to deliver library books, which gave him access to a large part of the cell house. While walking around Alcatraz, he began looking for weak points he could exploit. Coy found willing accomplices in fellow prisoners Joseph Cretzer, Marvin Hubbard, Sam Shockley, Miran Thompson, and Clarence Carnes.

On the afternoon of May 2, Coy and his coconspirators were able to overpower a guard and take his keys. They gagged the guard and tied him up in a cell. Their plan was to use a key to get into the recreation yard, kill the tower guards, take hostages, and use them to make their way to the dock. However, they quickly discovered they did not have the right key to open the recreation yard. Their plan started to unravel.

When other guards came to investigate, the prisoners ambushed them and threw them in cells too. Eventually, the armorer realized something was wrong. He called the warden and then sounded the alarm.

US Marines landed on the Rock armed with grenades and bayonets. Military planes flew overhead. Coast Guard boats circled the island. Officers circled the entire cell house and island.

A furious battle erupted. Gunfire and grenades exploded inside the prison. With weapons they had stolen from the guards, the inmates fired at any officers who tried to enter the prison. The officers they captured were shot at point-blank range. Cretzer swore they would never be taken alive.

On the morning of May 4, the sun rose on a bloody and battered Alcatraz prison. The exterior was covered in bullet holes and shattered windows. From inside the prison, there was silence. When officers entered the building, they found two guards and three prisoners—Coy, Cretzer, and Hubbard—dead. Eighteen officers were wounded. The Battle of Alcatraz was over.

Thompson, Shockley, and Carnes were tried for the murder of the two guards. Thompson and Shockley were given the death penalty and executed in 1948. Carnes, who was only 19 at the time, had his sentence extended to two life terms plus 99 years.

Final Escape Attempts

After the Battle of Alcatraz, more than a decade passed without another serious escape attempt. Then, on September 29, 1958, robbers Clyde Johnson and Aaron Burgett made a run for it while working garbage detail. They bound and gagged a guard. Using a blown-up bag as a flotation device, they tried to swim for shore.

Half an hour later, a Coast Guard boat picked up Johnson shivering in the water, his teeth chattering. He said, "We made a good try, but it just didn't work."[5] Nearly two weeks later, Burgett's body was found floating approximately 100 yards (91 m) off Alcatraz.

Four years later, another escape attempt would be much better planned and executed. In fact, it was so well planned that the inmates might just have gotten away with it.

Soldier or Prisoner?

One of the most ingenious escape attempts took place on July 31, 1945. Convicted robber John K. Giles was working on the loading dock one morning when an army boat, pulled up. The soldiers dropped off their laundry to be cleaned at the prison, and the boat pulled away. The prison guard then checked his men and found Giles was gone.

How had Giles escaped? While unloading army laundry, Giles had been able to collect an entire sergeant's uniform. On July 31, he was wearing that uniform under his work clothes. Giles hid in the boat's bathroom until it pushed off from the dock. He hoped it was headed for San Francisco and freedom. Instead, he was caught and returned to Alcatraz.

Chapter 6

The Players

Four men were involved in the Alcatraz escape plot. Three managed to get away. One stayed behind. Here are the stories of how all four came to be at Alcatraz.

Player #1—Frank Lee Morris

Frank Lee Morris was a smart, handsome guy with dark wavy hair and hazel eyes. Much of Morris's personal history is murky. His birth date is listed as September 1, 1926, although that is uncertain. Morris was born to a teenage runaway mother who abandoned him soon after birth. He was shuttled from one foster home to another. By all accounts, Morris was a nice kid, but he had a way of getting into trouble. At just 14, he started stealing. Breaking a window and swiping jewelry and money from a home got him locked up at the National Training School for Boys, a juvenile correctional facility in Washington DC.

After his release, Morris frequently ended up back in prison. Robbery and narcotics possession earned him terms at the Florida State Penitentiary and Louisiana State Penitentiary. But Morris was wily, and every time the legal system locked him up, he found a way to escape. On April 29, 1955, while on work detail cutting sugarcane, he and fellow inmate Bill Martin successfully escaped from the Louisiana State Penitentiary. They disappeared for a few months and evaded capture. Then Morris decided to try something risky.

In 1955, he broke through a wall to get into the Bank of Slidell in Louisiana. Then he burned a hole through one of the bank

Many experts consider Morris to be the architect of the escape plan.

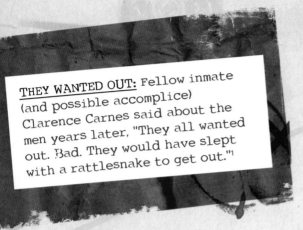

vaults and made off with $6,165. It might sound like an average bank robbery, but the entire take was in coins—1,200 pounds (544 kg) of coins. Police nabbed Morris in Louisiana, and he wound up with two sentences—14 years plus five years—at the Atlanta Federal Penitentiary. Once again, he tried to escape. Thanks to that attempt, he found himself on a train bound for Alcatraz.

Morris arrived at the Rock on January 20, 1960. He was 33 years old, and he had already spent nearly 20 years behind bars. Morris was assigned to cell B 138 on the bottom row of the B block.

Player #2—Allen West

In the cell next to Morris, B 140, lived Allen West, a Georgia native who had started his criminal career before he reached puberty. At age 11, he broke into a car. By 14, he was serving time in the Georgia State Farm for Boys. He was arrested nearly two dozen times and convicted of eight felonies, which included stabbings and a few prison escape attempts.

Allen West

For his crimes, he would spend time at the Georgia State Prison at Reidsville, the Florida State Prison at Raiford, the Atlanta Penitentiary, and the federal prison in Lewisburg, Pennsylvania.

When the escape plot took shape, West was already on his second term at Alcatraz, which had begun in June 1958. By all accounts, he was not a nice guy. He was a vicious racist, and Alcatraz guards described him as "belligerent," "sneaky," and "one of the most bitter, vicious, and criminally inclined person[s]" they had ever had to deal with.[2]

West had a history of trying to escape from prison. During one escape attempt from the Florida State Prison, he held a gun to the associate warden's head, stole his car keys, and escaped in the man's car. At Alcatraz, he talked constantly to the other inmates about taking hostages, stealing weapons, climbing through the ceiling vents to reach the roof, and using blown-up surgical gloves as water wings to swim for shore.

Players #3 and #4—John and Clarence Anglin

The Anglin brothers came from a family of 14 children. Their parents, George and Rachel Anglin, were poor farm workers in rural Ruskin, Florida. The older of the two brothers, John (also called J. W.), was blond-haired and blue-eyed. He was charming and talkative. Clarence, a year younger, was taller and heavier set, with dark hair and hazel-blue eyes.

THE POLITE STICK-UP: John and Clarence Anglin were charming—even as criminals. They reportedly held up an Alabama bank using toy pistols and politely asked for the cash. When a customer fainted, Clarence supposedly fanned her face until she came to.

John Anglin

As teens, John and Clarence worked menial jobs. John got a job at the Tropicana orange juice company making $1.25 an hour. According to the company, he was passed over for a promotion because of his poor attendance and lack of skills. John also worked as a truck driver for the Ajax Oil Company in Tampa, Florida.

It was not long before the brothers turned to a life of crime. They started with a few minor thefts, which landed Clarence in reform school at age 14 and put his brother there approximately one year later. It was at reform school that they honed their escape skills, which they later tried out at various prisons. In 1958, John and Clarence, along with their brother Alfred, stuck up a bank in Columbia, Alabama. They escaped with approximately $19,000

Clarence Anglin

but were arrested only days later while hiding out in Hamilton, Ohio. That hold-up earned John ten years at Leavenworth Prison in Kansas. Clarence got 15 years.

After trying to escape from Leavenworth, John was transferred to Alcatraz in October 1960. Clarence arrived three months later, in January 1961. They were put in adjoining cells, John in B 150 and Clarence in B 152.

Escaping in a Bread Box

John and Clarence Anglin worked on their escape skills over many years. By the time they were sentenced to terms at Leavenworth Prison, they were pretty good at it.

Clarence decided to hatch a creative escape plan. While working in the prison bakery, he cut the top out of one big metal bread box and the bottom out of another. He and John hid inside, covered with loaves of bread. Just as the boxes were about to be loaded on a truck and shipped out, a prison officer caught movement coming from one of the boxes and the men were caught.

Chapter 7

The Plan

Morris, West, and the Anglins did not decide to escape from Alcatraz on the spur of the moment. They thought about and planned it for more than a year.

After the escape, investigators wondered which one of them had masterminded the plot. It became a matter of some debate. Though West claimed responsibility for the idea, he was the only one left behind to tell his story, and he was a known braggart. Experts say that with West's eighth-grade education, he probably would not have been able to concoct a plan as sophisticated as the one the men executed. Morris was the one with the high IQ and a history of staging sophisticated escapes. Plus, investigators found articles on how to make life jackets and boats in Morris's cell—not West's.

The Idea

Whoever devised the plan, it started with a ventilator shaft. There were eight of these ventilators in the prison ceiling, but only one of them was not cemented closed. Once the four men learned about it, they realized that if they could somehow climb up to the top of the prison and remove the ventilator cover, they could get out onto the prison roof.

While they pondered how to get to the ventilator shaft, Morris kept a careful watch over the guards and their routines. He clocked when and how often they did their rounds and when they took breaks.

West was also taking in some very valuable information. While he was assigned to the job of cleaning up after the plumbing crew that was installing hot water faucets in the cells, he got a rare look inside the utility corridor behind the

ABOVE AVERAGE: By most estimates, Morris had an IQ of 133. The average person has an IQ of approximately 100.

The escapees improvised many tools, including this homemade wrench.

cells. He discovered water and heating pipes that conveniently reached all the way to the top of the cell house. West thought they would make a great ladder. In addition to information, West gathered tools such as drill bits and used saw blades while on work detail.

Soon, the Anglins, whom Morris and West already knew from their time at other prisons, were brought into the plot. Whenever they had a chance to be together in the recreation yard or mess hall, the men worked out the details of their plan. Shortly after, their focus turned to the tiny air vents in the back of their cells. If they could just figure out a way to break them open, they would have access to the utility corridor. From there, they could make their way to the cell house roof.

Digging

Those tiny air vents could be their ticket to freedom, but how would they open them up without any tools or any of the guards noticing? Morris's first thought was to burn through the concrete. He had read that when concrete is heated up, it crumbles. The men tried to melt the concrete by creating heat with an electric cord attached to the cell's ceiling light socket. It did not work. They realized they would have to dig the vent open.

At night, the men began chipping away at

Digging Tools

Digging through the 8-inch- (20-cm-) thick concrete at the back of the cells was slow and laborious. Morris knew he needed a real tool if he was going to dig faster. The only option was to make that tool himself.

Morris shaved some silver off a dime and melted it using the heat from several lit matches. That melted silver created a solder, which Morris used to connect the handle of his nail clipper to a spoon he had stolen from the mess hall. Together, the clipper handle and spoon formed a rudimentary pick. It worked! The digging proceeded much more quickly.

Even with Morris's ingenuity, experts question whether all four men could have dug such big holes through the concrete wall of their cells using only spoons and handmade tools. Various real tools were also found in the men's cells, including drill bits and pieces of saws. It is possible those items were also used to dig.

the concrete around each of their cell vents using the sharpened ends of spoons they had stolen from the mess hall. They created tiny holes, which they eventually combined to form bigger and bigger holes. The men did their digging during Happy Hour, between 5:30 and 9:30 p.m. The sound of the other inmates playing their instruments drowned out the noise of their work.

The men took turns looking out for one another. Morris worked while West pointed a mirror down the hall to watch for guards. The Anglins ran a piece of string between their cells. When one brother spotted a guard, he wiggled the string to alert the other brother.

As Morris crumbled away more and more of the concrete around his vent, he had to find ways to get rid of it. He threw some of the concrete chips in the toilet, put some in his pockets, and took the rest outside when he went to work. Eventually the hole was big enough to hide the dug out concrete inside it.

Once the men had made a few holes in their vents, another problem surfaced: how would they hide the holes? At first, Morris used wet toilet paper smoothed over with soap chips to cover them. But as the men loosened more and more cement and the holes grew larger, he knew he needed something bigger to fill them. Morris collected magazines that were distributed from the library. Ripping out the pages and wetting them, he created a sort of paste. The men placed the paste over the holes, and then painted it to match the wall using paint they bought from the prison.

After many nights of digging, the concrete was finally loose enough for Morris to pull out the grill. But that left a gaping hole—yet

Paint Test

After the escape, the FBI dug out the material that filled the holes around the air vents in the men's cells. They found a mixture of soap and paper covered by a green-colored paint. In addition, the paint bottles shown here were found in the prisoners' cells.

The FBI took a paint sample and performed a test called spectrochemical analysis. This technique helps scientists discover the chemical properties of an object. Using visual color tests and X-rays, they can see how the substance absorbs radiation, and this helps tell them what it is made from.

The FBI discovered the paint Morris and the Anglins used to cover the holes in their cell walls was the same cement paint the prison had purchased in 1961. It is possible that West stole the paint while working in the prison.

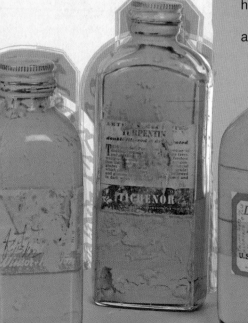

DO NOT OPEN
EVIDENCE!
FOR LABORATORY
FEDERAL BUREAU OF INVESTIGATION
U.S. DEPARTMENT OF JUSTICE
WASHINGTON, D. C.

another problem. Luckily, Morris had yet another solution. Using pieces of cardboard from the prison art supplies, he cut out a rectangle the exact size and shape of the grill. On it, he drew the precise crisscross pattern of the grill and painted it the same shade of green. He attached a backing to create a box with the fake grill in front. When he was finished digging each night, he could simply slide the entire fake grill into place. Each escapee did the same with the grill in his cell.

Morris filled in the gaps around the edges of the replacement grill using soap modeled with pits

One of the false grills the escapees used to hide the holes in their cells

to look like the cell's concrete wall. It looked almost exactly like the real thing, but just to be safe, Morris left his concertina case in front of the vent. John Anglin hung a long raincoat in front of it. The guards noticed nothing.

Decoys—Oink and Oscar

The grills were finally big enough for the men to squeeze through, but they could not just leave their cells empty and climb to the top of the cell house. They needed decoys.

To make models of themselves required some creativity and a fair amount of artistic talent, which the Anglins possessed. It also required hair, which Clarence Anglin was able to steal from his job at the prison barbershop.

The first dummy head the Anglins made was constructed of rags covered with soap. It was not a whole head—just a profile with an eye, nose, and ear that they painted a flesh color. Clarence added the hair he stole from the barbershop to the top of the head and used it to form eyebrows and eyelashes. The half-head was so ugly the men jokingly called it "Oink."[1] Next came "Oscar," a more complete and human looking head molded out of toilet paper and soap to form a homemade plaster. Because it had dark, wavy hair, Oscar became Morris's decoy.

Clarence Anglin's decoy head was finished only on the side that would show in the bed.

When the men sneaked out of their cells to work at the top of the cell house, they left the dummy heads on their pillows and stuffed rolled-up blankets and clothes under the covers to form the shape of their bodies. The dummies looked so realistic that

the guards who were patrolling the B block never
even paused for a second look.

A Secret Industry

While prison life went on as usual, Morris, West,
and the Anglins were creating a whole other industry
inside Alcatraz. From their jobs, they were able to
steal all kinds of supplies—surplus navy raincoats
from the clothing room in the prison basement and
saw blades, scrap metal, plywood, and glue from
the shops where they worked. Some of the materials
they ordered from the prison, including art supplies,
magazines, and a concertina.

Once the men were free from their cells, they
were able to climb up the ladder of pipes and
ductwork to the top of the cell house, where there
was a little space.
There, they made
their very own
workshop where they
assembled all of the
tools they would need
to escape.

To get off
Alcatraz, they would
have to survive the
frigid waters of

MAKE-IT-YOURSELF FLASHLIGHT:
Morris was industrious. When he
needed a light to see up into
the ventilator shaft, he made
his own flashlight out of two
penlight batteries inside a small
rectangular plastic box with a
bulb at one end. A metal fastener
carried the electricity from the
battery to the bulb and acted as a
switch.

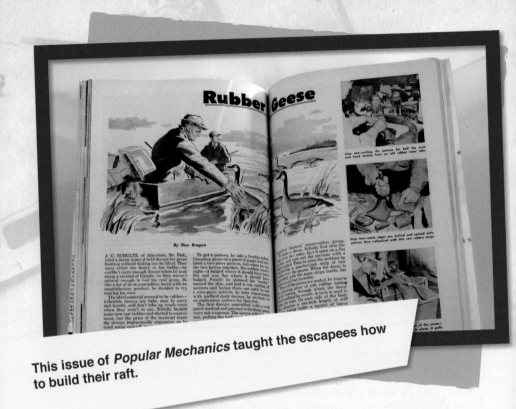

This issue of *Popular Mechanics* taught the escapees how to build their raft.

the bay, which meant they would need boats and flotation devices. Morris had read an article in *Popular Mechanics* magazine that taught him how to make a life jacket. He constructed the life jacket—as well as pontoon rafts—using the waterproof navy raincoats they had stolen—55 of them in all.

To construct the life jackets, the men folded the bottom of the raincoats and glued a long strap of canvas along the fold. Then they glued two panels together at the top and sides of the raincoats to form a large air-filled sac. To seal the glue, the men used hot steam from pipes. At the top of this sac they left a hole big enough for their head to fit through. The air-filled sac would sit on their chest, with straps that tied around their back. They added a tube taken from a Windex bottle so the wearer could blow into it if the vest started to deflate. A paper clip went around the tube and sealed it off so air could not escape.

They also constructed a six by 14 foot (2 by 4 m) rubber raft out of raincoats. To inflate the raft, Morris removed the keys from the concertina he bought from the prison and used it as a bellows. When he squeezed the concertina, it would release a stream of air to blow up the raft. To steer the raft, Morris crafted wooden paddles in the shop where he worked. They also fashioned a spare raft that investigators later found left behind on the prison roof.

VULCANIZED RUBBER: To strengthen the life vests and rafts, Morris used a process invented by Charles Goodyear in the 1830s. Called vulcanization, this process uses heat to strengthen rubber and make it more resistant to tears.

The First Trip Up

In the spring of 1962, Clarence Anglin was the first person to climb the pipes to the top of the cell house to reach the ceiling vent. What he discovered was disheartening. The ventilator—their route out of Alcatraz—was covered with a cap attached by solid metal screws. Clarence tried using a wrench made with clasps taken from his bed, but he could not loosen them by hand. They needed to find an electric drill.

West managed to steal an electric hair clipper. He fashioned a makeshift drill by attaching stolen drill bits. Morris tried to use this drill to open the bolts, but it was too small and weak. They needed a stronger motor.

That request also fell to West. When he learned the prison's vacuum cleaner had broken, he offered to fix it. Much to his surprise and delight, he discovered that inside it was not one, but two motors. West fixed one motor and removed the other. To this motor he attached drill bits. Wrapping a thick strip of cloth around the new drill to muffle its noise, Morris set to work on the screws. But almost as soon as he started, the motor blew out.

Morris decided he would have to work on the screws by hand, using a screwdriver to jiggle them out of place. The work was slow, but eventually he was able to wriggle the screws free. He replaced each screw he removed with a fake one modeled out of soap.

On the night of Sunday, June 10, Morris sent word out to the rest of the men: the last screw was free. It was time to go.

West used this vacuum cleaner motor to power a drill.

Chapter 8

Breaking Out

On the night of June 11, 1962, most of the work was finished. The men now had a clear route to the top of the cell house. The screws that attached the cap of the ventilator had been loosened. All that was left was to open a few bars at the top of the ventilator shaft—their last obstacle to reaching the roof.

After the lights went out for the night at 9:30 p.m., the Anglin brothers and Morris placed the dummies in their beds, sneaked out of their cells, and went up to the vent. Morris came back down and told West he had pried open the bars leading to the roof. The flotation devices and rolled up rafts, as well as the wooden oars Morris had made, were waiting next to the ventilator shaft. They were clear to go.

Soon after, Clarence appeared at the back of West's cell. Of the four men, West was the only one who had not quite finished opening the hole in the back of his cell. There was still some cement remaining around the edges that had to be removed before the hole would be big enough for West to wriggle through. Clarence tried breaking open the hole from behind the wall while West worked at it from inside his cell. Morris brought West a piece of pipe to hit the cement with, but it made too much noise. West started to panic but kept digging.

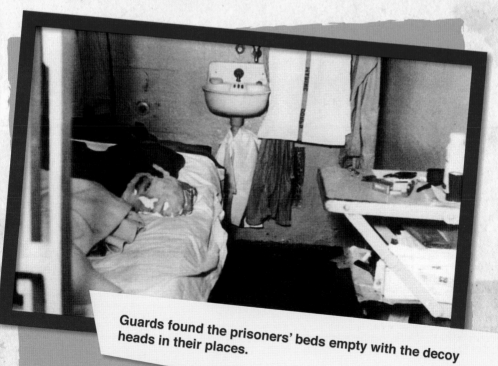

Guards found the prisoners' beds empty with the decoy heads in their places.

Meanwhile, the Anglin brothers were getting antsy. They did not want to miss their opportunity to escape. The brothers and Morris left West to his fate and continued according to plan.

Getting Out

At around 10:30 p.m., Morris pulled open the cap to the roof vent. As was typical for Alcatraz, it was cold and windy that night. A gust of wind pulled the cap from his hands and it went clattering to the roof. The loud noise scared the seagulls on the roof, sending them into the air in a chattering clamor.

Inside the west gun gallery, an officer heard the noise. "It sounded like a person hitting the end of an empty fifty-gallon oil drum with the heel of his hand," he later wrote.[1] The officer reported the noise to the lieutenant on duty, who went to investigate inside the prison. He found nothing.

Meanwhile, Morris was easing himself up the shaft to the roof. John Anglin passed him the life vest, paddles, rafts, and other accessories. John pulled himself to the roof and then helped Clarence up. They ran across the roof. In their haste, they dropped one of their wooden paddles. They left behind a spare life vest and the spare raft.

At the other end of the roof, they climbed down a pipe approximately 45 feet (14 m) down the outside wall of the prison kitchen. As John went down, he swung a little too hard, causing the pipe to bang against the wall. Another loud noise cut through the silent night. Guards later reported hearing the noise at 10:30 or 10:45 p.m.

The three men crawled across an open space to reach a 14-foot (4-m) fence topped with barbed wire. They scaled the fence and then crept along beside the prison yard. They climbed another fence and then went down a steep hill to the road. The men ran across the road and down another steep slope to the northeast shore of the island.

By 11:00 p.m., Morris and the Anglins had probably reached the water's edge. They rolled out the raft and fitted the concertina into the hole so they could inflate it. Then they inflated the life preservers and slid them over their heads, tying them in the back.

Next, the three men waded out into the water. They loaded all of their supplies into the

The escapees created these wooden paddles. One paddle was dropped during the escape attempt; the other was recovered in San Francisco Bay.

Conditions on the Bay

On the night of June 11, 1962, as Morris and the Anglins were pushing off into San Francisco Bay, there was a swift tide. By some estimates, it was flowing as fast as seven miles per hour (11 km/h). The way the tide was flowing, it would have naturally pushed the raft west toward the Golden Gate Bridge and out toward the Pacific Ocean, instead of north toward their intended destination, Angel Island. The men would have had to paddle pretty hard, which would have been difficult, especially since they had dropped one paddle while running across the roof.

When the men pushed off, the water temperature was between 50 and 54 degrees Fahrenheit (10 and 12°C). Immersed at that temperature, the average person would begin to grow very tired within an hour. After three hours, experts say the men would have developed hypothermia, and they would have been unlikely to survive.

raft, climbed aboard, and pushed off into the blackness.

Left Behind

West continued to dig furiously at the back of his cell. Finally, at around 1:45 a.m., he was able to break through.

When the guards took a break from their late-night rounds, he climbed up the utility corridor pipes and into the ventilator shaft. He put on his life jacket and hoisted himself to the roof. It was empty.

West stood there for a few moments. He was possibly thinking of what could have been. Then he climbed back down the shaft, crawled back into his cell, and got into bed. He had been left behind.

This spare raft was made from raincoats sewn together and then heated to seal them. Investigators found it on the roof after the escape attempt, along with a life vest of similar construction. Two other life vests were found in the waters around Alcatraz.

When one of the officers walked through the B block early in the morning hours to make his routine check, he unknowingly included three dummies in his count. At the moment he was passing their cells, the three men whose beds they occupied were likely navigating the waters of San Francisco Bay.

Chapter 9

The Investigation

At 7:15 a.m. on the morning of June 12, Officer Lawrence "Sarge" Bartlett did his routine head count along the B block. When he tried to wake a "sleeping" Clarence Anglin, the prisoner would not budge. He ran down Broadway yelling, "Bill, Bill, I got one I can't wake up!"[1]

He was calling for Lieutenant Bill Long, who ran the cell block during the midnight-to-morning shift. Long went down to Anglin's cell to investigate Bartlett's claim. He got down on one knee in front of the cell and put his head up against the bar. "I reached my left hand in through the bars and hit the pillow and hollered,

'Get up for the count!'" Long later recalled. "Bam, the head flopped off on the floor. . . . They said I jumped four feet back from the bars."[2] An officer in front of Morris's cell yelled, "I got one here too!"[3] Long ran to the phone and the alarm was sounded.

The Search Begins

A massive search was launched—in the air, on the ground, and in the water. The US Coast Guard sent out a helicopter and patrol boats, which skimmed the waters of the bay from Alcatraz and Angel Island to the San Francisco piers and Golden Gate Bridge, looking for any trace of the men. The California Highway Patrol checked cars in the area.

Law enforcement officials searched San Francisco Bay by boat.

One hundred soldiers from the 561st Engineering Company at Fort Baker searched Angel Island, approximately two miles (3 km) north of Alcatraz, looking for any sign of the convicts.

FBI agencies in several states received a message with detailed descriptions of the three men. They received pictures later.

FBI special agents patrolled the San Francisco shoreline, interviewing people who lived and worked there. Agents conducted a door-to-door search in Sausalito and Tiburon, two coastal towns in the area. Divers searched the depths of the waters around Alcatraz.

Meanwhile, back on Alcatraz, officers scoured the island and searched the cell house from top to bottom. At the top of the cell house, they discovered the workshop where the four men had worked for months to execute their escape plan. They found rubber raincoat material, glue, a homemade periscope the men had used to peer up through the vent to the roof, and scraps of metal. An officer discovered a five-gallon can of white cement paint that had solidified. When he cracked the paint, the officer found inside several sharpened spoon handles, pieces of metal and wire, and a screw.

Investigators examine the area behind Clarence's cell, B 152. The prisoners escaped through this utility area.

In the three men's cells they found the dummy heads and the magazine articles detailing how to make rafts and life vests. Under Morris's bed, they found saw blades. The FBI analyzed the blades to find out how old they were and which company had manufactured them. They turned out to be homemade.

Up on the roof, investigators found the wooden paddle the men had left behind, as well as a life vest and the spare raft. Officers followed the men's shoeprints across to the west side of the roof. The same footprints were also at the bottom of the pipe that ran down the side of the prison wall.

Bloodhounds were brought in to follow the men's trail. It led down the hill, across the road, and down another hill to the water's edge. There the scent stopped.

Piecing Together the Plot

A big part of the FBI's investigation involved interviews, and their best witness was West, who had been in on the plot. In fact, West claimed responsibility for planning the escape. He was more than willing to share everything he knew with the FBI because he was bitter at having been left behind.

West said the plan had been to paddle north to Angel Island, rest, and then get back into the bay on the opposite side of the island. After swimming through a waterway called Raccoon Straits, they planned to reach the shores of Marin County. There, they would steal a car, rob a clothing store, and each head off in their

WEST TALKS: When West was taken to the A Block and interviewed by prison officials, he reportedly "bubbled over" with information.[4] He said he planned the escape and made the life jackets and paddles. West seemed to like all the attention he was getting from investigators.

The FBI issued this wanted poster for John Anglin.

own separate directions. Officers followed up on this lead, looking into every Northern California robbery for weeks. None of the burglaries could be linked to the fugitives.

FBI agents also interviewed other prisoners, including men who had recently been released from Alcatraz. All of them denied involvement in the plot. Interviews were also done with relatives of the

Anglins. None of them had seen the brothers for many years.

Following Leads

Over the next few weeks, several important clues were found. The FBI followed up on each one.

June 12—A homemade wooden paddle matching the one used by the escapees was found floating approximately 100 yards (91 m) off Angel Island.

June 13—A woman from San Rafael called the police, claiming to have seen a raft with three men aboard floating approximately ten miles (16 km) north of Alcatraz. When the FBI investigated, the three men turned out to be fishermen.

June 14—A US Corps of Engineers debris boat, which constantly swept the bay for trash, fished out of the water a packet made out of raincoat material. Inside it were several sheets of paper and 79 photos, which featured the Anglins and some of their friends and relatives. The papers contained names and addresses of contacts on shore, as well as the name of an attorney who had defended Alcatraz inmates in the past.

June 15—A man and his wife were walking along Cronkhite Beach, approximately one mile (2 km) west of the Golden Gate Bridge, when they saw an object floating 50 feet (15 m) from shore. When it washed ashore, they took it to police. It was the same kind of life jacket the escapees had made. The FBI searched the area, but they found nothing more.

June 18—A postcard addressed to "Warden Alcatraz Prison, Alcatraz Island, San Francisco Bay, California," was received at the prison. On it was written, "HA HA WE MADE IT." It was signed "Frank, John, Clarence."[5] The handwriting was compared to documents written by Morris and

The escapees made it out of the ventilator shaft and off the prison roof. But did they make it to safety?

the Anglins. The handwriting analysis proved that Clarence could not have written the postcard, but it was unclear whether one of the other two men might have written it. The postcard was also examined for fingerprints, but nothing useful was found.

June 22—Officers spotted another life jacket bobbing approximately 100 yards off the east side of Alcatraz. It had brown stains on it that looked like blood, but when the FBI analyzed them, it was not blood. Tooth marks were found on the dipstick inflation tube—a sign that whoever was wearing the life jacket had been trying to keep it inflated. The ties used to fasten the life jacket were still knotted at the back.

June 26—The FBI received a letter from a 73-year-old

Handwriting Analysis

When Morris and the Anglins escaped in the 1960s, the FBI had few sophisticated investigation tools, such as computers and scanners, at its disposal. One very basic technique they did have was handwriting analysis.

The idea behind handwriting analysis is that each person has his or her own unique style of writing. Comparing a handwriting sample from a known author to a sample from an unknown author provides evidence whether the person in question wrote the sample.

During a handwriting analysis, the investigator looks very closely at the size and shape of the letters, how dark and smooth they are (which determines how much pressure the person put on the pen or pencil), and how much space there is between letters, words, and lines.

woman who lived on a farm in Lincoln, Nebraska. She said a man tied her up and held her captive on the night of June 18, making off with her watch, diamond ring, and $75 in cash. The man claimed he had just escaped

Testing the Life Jackets

The FBI found three of the fugitives' life jackets after the escape, and they wanted to know how far the men could have gotten while wearing them. To test their water resistance, the FBI reinflated the life jackets and then put weights on them as pressure. Ironically, the life jacket the men had left behind stayed airtight. Both of the jackets that were found in the water lost air within an hour, but the leak was slow enough that the men could have kept themselves afloat by blowing into the dipstick.

from Alcatraz. When FBI agents arrived to interview the woman, her story fell apart and her description did not match any of the fugitives.

Chapter 10

Did They Make It?

Ultimately, Alcatraz became too expensive to maintain. On March 21, 1963, the government abandoned it as a federal prison and the prisoners were sent to other facilities. Today, Alcatraz is a major tourist destination that hosts more than 1.5 million visitors a year.

Many people travel there because they are fascinated by the story of the Alcatraz escape, and they wonder what happened to Morris and the Anglin brothers. Investigators are still pondering that very same question.

The last prisoners were removed from Alcatraz on March 21, 1963.

Numerous Sightings

Over the years, Morris and the Anglins were allegedly spotted many times. They were seen in bars from Seattle, Washington, to Dodge City, Kansas. Morris was supposedly living in New Orleans, Louisiana, under the name Frankie Lyons. He might have also been in Silver Spring, Maryland. John Anglin might have worked at Grossinger's Resort in the Catskill Mountains of New York—or he might have been the same man who cashed a check for $25 at the Red and White Food Store in Brundidge, Alabama.

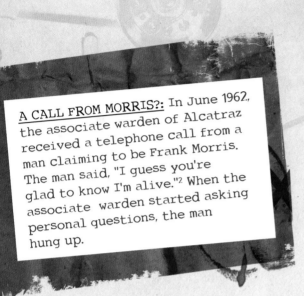

In June 1962, the associate warden of Alcatraz received a telephone call from a man claiming to be Frank Morris. The man said, "I guess you're glad to know I'm alive."[2] When the associate warden started asking personal questions, the man hung up.

Every time the FBI followed up on a lead—and officers did follow up every lead—it turned into a dead end.

Could They Survive?

One of the biggest keys to the three men's survival would have been their ability to make it to shore. Many experts believe there is no way they made it. Shortly after the escape, Assistant Director Fred T. Wilkinson from the Federal Bureau of Prisons said, "The tides and winds that night were strong, [and] these convicts were not the athletic type. Only a trained athlete could make such a swim."[1] Yet several people have made the very same swim since then, including a couple of grade-school children, proving that it would not have been impossible. The children's wet suits gave them a large advantage over the escapees, however.

One important piece of evidence that may point to the three men's deaths surfaced on July 17,

1962. The *Norefjell*, a Norwegian ship, was approximately 20 miles (32 km) west-northwest of the Golden Gate Bridge when one of its sailors spotted a body floating in the water. It was wearing what looked like prison-issued pants. Although the

MYTHBUSTERS: In 2003, the television show *Mythbusters* tested whether the escapees could have made it to shore. The crew constructed a raft following the prisoners' model and successfully rode it from Alcatraz to shore. The experiment showed that it was possible to escape from the island in such a raft, although the prisoners would have been operating at night and guessing about the tide and the best direction to take.

chief officer noted the sighting in the ship's log, he did not report it because they were on their way to Canada and did not have a radio. When the *Norefjell* returned to the United States the following month, the officer told the FBI about the sighting, but by then it was too late. The body was never found.

On October 15, 1963, a memo to the FBI director from the San Francisco FBI office summarizing the investigation so far wrote, "Exhaustive investigation has failed to offer any scintilla of evidence indicating that Escapees ever reached the mainland from Alcatraz."[3]

Yet other evidence makes the three men's fate less certain. Old FBI files mention a raft was found on Angel Island, but no further information exists or has been released to the public. If the men made it to Angel Island, their chances of reaching the mainland were much higher.

What Happens to Bodies in the Bay?

If Morris and the Anglins drowned during their escape, would their bodies have floated to the surface and been found? Not necessarily.

A body can take one or two weeks to float to the surface, or it may never emerge at all. Whether a body floats or sinks depends on many factors including the water temperature, air temperature, weather conditions, tides, the person's weight, and what he or she ate recently.

A body rises because of gases trapped inside. Bacteria produce these gases. When it is cold in the water or air, bacteria have a hard time surviving, so gases do not form as quickly. Crabs and other marine life can also break open the body and release the gases, forcing it to sink. Swift tides can sweep a body out to sea or a body can become trapped on plant life at the bottom of the water. In all of these cases, the body may never rise to the surface.

On November 30, 1993, an interview with former bank robber Thomas Kent aired on *America's Most Wanted*. Kent claimed he was in on the breakout. He added new details about the escape, saying that Clarence Anglin had arranged for an old girlfriend to meet them on the shores of Tiburon and drive them to Mexico.

From there, they were headed to South America. FBI records do show that Morris had bought a Berlitz teach-yourself-Spanish book. Dave Branham, a spokesman for the US Marshals Service said of the interview, "It gives strong credence to the probability that they did escape."[4]

If the men did survive, why did they not contact any friends or family members? Maybe they did. Some members of the Anglin family have reported receiving unsigned postcards and Christmas cards. At an Anglin family funeral, a couple of unknown and heavily made-up "women" were spotted. Could they have been John and Clarence in disguise?

Former inmate Darwin Coon was one of the last prisoners at Alcatraz and a friend of the escapees.

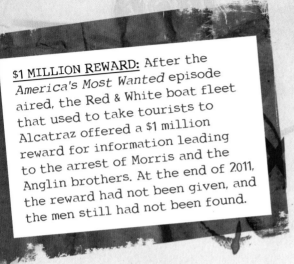

$1 MILLION REWARD: After the *America's Most Wanted* episode aired, the Red & White boat fleet that used to take tourists to Alcatraz offered a $1 million reward for information leading to the arrest of Morris and the Anglin brothers. At the end of 2011, the reward had not been given, and the men still had not been found.

Case Closed?

By the mid-1960s, the trail of Morris and the Anglins had grown cold. Despite many leads, there had been no definite sighting of the three men. In 1970, Rachel Anglin, John and Clarence's mother, asked a lawyer to start proceedings to pronounce her sons dead.

Though the FBI vowed, "The case is not closed until there is a body," they closed the file on the Alcatraz case in 1979.[5] The US Marshals Service in San Francisco took over, and it continues to investigate the Alcatraz escape today. Deputy US Marshall Michael Dyke is in charge of the case. He still gets leads and still follows up on them. "There's no proof they're dead, so we're not going to quit looking," he says.[6]

When Morris and the Anglins slipped into the water, their trail went cold. There were no signs of stolen cars or boats they might have used to escape. There were no burglaries to prove they stole money or supplies to survive. And there were no proven sightings of the three men.

What does Dyke think happened to the three men? He ran tests of the escape with the Coast Guard, and the evidence showed the men could have survived in the water for two and a half hours if their boat sank. Because they had an eight- to ten-hour lead, it is quite possible they stole a car and made it out of the country. "Sometimes I hope—I hope they did escape, because then I can catch them," Dyke said.[7] If he were still alive in 2011, Frank Morris would be 85. John and Clarence Anglin would be 81 and 80 years old.

Today, tourists come and go freely from Alcatraz.

Tools and Clues

digging tools— Morris and the Anglins sharpened the ends of spoons and used them to dig. Morris melted silver and used it to attach a spoon to the handle of his nail clipper. Together, the clipper handle and spoon formed a rudimentary pick.

drill— The men made a makeshift drill out of drill bits attached to a stolen vacuum cleaner motor.

dummies— The Anglins created dummy heads out of toilet paper and soap, with human hair stolen from the prison barbershop.

fake grill covers— Morris and the Anglins made covers to hide the holes they had dug in the back of their cells.

handwriting analysis— The FBI compared the handwriting on a note sent to the Alcatraz warden with samples taken from the escapees to see if it was a match.

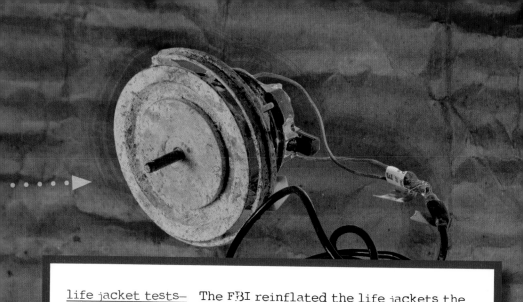

life jacket tests—	The FBI reinflated the life jackets the escapees had made and put weights on them to test their water resistance.
life jackets—	The men made life jackets out of raincoats, which they sealed using the heat from steam coming off the prison pipes. A tube taken from a Windex bottle allowed the wearer to inflate the vest.
spectrochemical analysis—	The FBI used this technique to compare the paint Morris and the Anglins had used to cover the holes in their cell walls to find out if it matched the cement paint the prison had purchased in 1961.

Timeline

1775   Spanish naval lieutenant Don Juan Manuel de Ayala discovers and names the island La Isla de los Alcatraces, or the Island of the Pelicans.

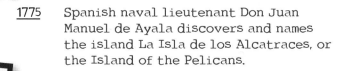

1853   Construction of the Alcatraz fortress begins.

1934   Alcatraz is turned into a federal prison on January 1.

1934   The first group of prisoners arrives at Alcatraz on August 11.

1936   Joseph Bowers attempts to scale a fence and escape from Alcatraz in August.

1937   Ralph Roe and Theodore Cole slip into the waters off Alcatraz and disappear on December 16.

1938   James C. Lucas, Rufus Franklin, and Thomas R. Limerick kill a guard while trying to escape on May 23.

1939   On January 13, five prisoners, including Arthur "Doc" Barker, attempt to escape. Guards kill Barker and return the other four inmates to their cells.

1945   On July 31, John K. Giles tries to escape from the Alcatraz docks wearing a stolen military uniform.

1946   Bernard Paul Coy leads the bloody Battle of Alcatraz from May 2 to May 4.

Timeline

1958   Allen West arrives in June for his second stint at Alcatraz.

1958   Clyde Johnson and Aaron Burgett try to escape on September 29; Johnson is caught in the bay and Burgett's body is found two weeks later.

1960   Frank Lee Morris arrives at Alcatraz on January 20.

1960   John Anglin is transferred to Alcatraz in October.

1961   Clarence Anglin arrives at Alcatraz in January.

1962   Frank Lee Morris and John and Clarence Anglin escape from Alcatraz on June 11.

1962   On June 12, a homemade paddle similar to that made by the escapees is found floating off the coast of Angel Island.

1962   On June 14, a US Corps of Engineers boat finds a packet made out of raincoat material containing photographs of the Anglins and a list of names and addresses.

1962   On June 15, a couple finds one of the fugitives' life jackets along Cronkhite Beach. Another life jacket is found on June 22.

1962   The S.S. *Norefjell* spots a body floating in the water approximately 20 miles (32 km) from the Golden Gate Bridge on July 17.

1963   The federal prison at Alcatraz closes in March.

1979   The FBI closes its case on the Alcatraz escape and the US Marshals Service office in San Francisco takes over.

Glossary

arsenal. . . . . A collection of weapons.

bellows . . . . A device that contains a bag that releases air when squeezed.

bootlegging . . . . Making, selling, or distributing illegal liquor.

catwalk . . . . A narrow walkway.

citadel . . . . A fortress that protects an area of land.

concertina . . . . A musical instrument that is played by pulling outward and collapsing inward between the hands, similar to an accordion.

felony . . . . A serious and often violent crime that is punishable by a prison sentence.

<u>gun gallery</u>........	An enclosed cage that ran around the perimeter of Alcatraz, where an armed guard would patrol.
<u>hacksaw</u>	A fine-toothed saw used for cutting metal.
<u>hypothermia</u>.......	A condition that occurs when the body temperature drops dangerously low.
<u>incarcerated</u>	Kept locked up in a prison.
<u>mess hall</u>.........	A large room where groups of prisoners eat together.
<u>solder</u>	A type of heated metal used to join together two pieces of metal.
<u>solitary</u>..........	An area of prison that keeps an inmate apart from others.
<u>ventilator</u> .... <u>shaft</u>	An open passageway that allows fresh air to enter a building.

Additional Resources

Selected Bibliography

Babyak, Jolene. Breaking *The Rock*. Berkeley, CA: Ariel Vamp, 2001. Print.

Bruce, J. Campbell. *Escape From Alcatraz*. New York: McGraw-Hill, 2005. Print.

Esslinger, Michael. *Alcatraz: A Definitive History of the Penitentiary Years*. Carmel, CA: Ocean View, 2003. Print.

FBI. *John Anglin, Clarence Anglin and Frank Lee Morris Escape from Alcatraz*. File number 76-26295. Volume number 1. Web. 22 May 2011.

"Mystery Still Swirls Around Alcatraz Escape." *NPR.com*. NPR, 21 Sep 2009. Web. 17 May 2011.

Further Readings

Sloate, Susan. *Mysteries Unwrapped: The Secrets of Alcatraz*. New York: Sterling, 2008. Print.

Vercillo, Kathryn. *Ghosts of Alcatraz*. Atglen, PA: Schiffer, 2008. Print.

Wellman, Gregory. *History of Alcatraz Island, 1853–2008*. Charleston, SC: Arcadia, 2008. Print.

Web Links

To learn more about the escape from Alcatraz, visit ABDO Publishing Company online at **www.abdopublishing.com**. Web sites about the escape from Alcatraz are featured on our Book Links page. These links are routinely monitored and updated to provide the most current information available.

Places to Visit

Alcatraz Island
Golden Gate National Recreation Area
Fort Mason, B201
San Francisco, CA 94123
415-981-7625
http://www.nps.gov/alca/index.htm
Alcatraz is now a tourist destination run by the National Park
Service. Visitors can walk through Alcatraz prison, reliving its
history and viewing the cells from which Morris and the Anglins
escaped.

National Museum of Crime & Punishment
575 Seventh Street NW
Washington, D.C. 20004
202-393-1099
http://www.crimemuseum.org/
Visitors can learn firsthand how crimes are investigated by touring
this museum's interactive crime labs and other exhibits.

Source Notes

Chapter 1. Escape from the Rock

1. J. Campbell Bruce. *Escape From Alcatraz*. New York: McGraw-Hill, 2005. Print. 7.

Chapter 2. The History of Alcatraz

1. J. Campbell Bruce. *Escape From Alcatraz*. New York: McGraw-Hill, 2005. Print. 23.

2. Ibid. 21.

Chapter 3. Life on the Rock

1. J. Campbell Bruce. *Escape From Alcatraz*. New York: McGraw-Hill, 2005. Print. 40.

Chapter 4. Security on Alcatraz

1. J. Campbell Bruce. *Escape From Alcatraz*. New York: McGraw-Hill, 2005. Print. 20.

2. Michael Esslinger. *Alcatraz: A Definitive History of the Penitentiary Years*. Carmel, CA: Ocean View Publishing, 2003. Print. 62.

Chapter 5. Escape Attempts

1. J. Campbell Bruce. *Escape From Alcatraz*. New York: McGraw-Hill, 2005. Print. 58.

2. Ibid. 60.

3. "Alcatraz Felon Killed, One Shot, Third Seized as Guards Foil Escape." *San Francisco Chronicle* 24 May 1938: 1, 5. Print.

4. J. Campbell Bruce. *Escape From Alcatraz*. New York: McGraw-Hill, 2005. Print. 64.

5. Ibid. 146.

Chapter 6. The Players

1. Jolene Babyak. *Breaking The Rock*. Berkeley, CA: Ariel Vamp Press, 2001. Print. 74.

2. Ibid. 42.

Chapter 7. The Plan

1. "John Anglin, Clarence Anglin and Frank Lee Morris Escape from Alcatraz." *FBI*. FBI, n.d. File number 76-26295. Volume number 3. Web. 23 May 2011.

Chapter 8. Breaking Out

1. Jolene Babyak. *Breaking The Rock*. Berkeley, CA: Ariel Vamp Press, 2001. Print. 210.

Chapter 9. The Investigation

1. Jolene Babyak. *Breaking The Rock*. Berkeley, CA: Ariel Vamp Press, 2001. Print. 219.

2. "Escape From Alcatraz and a 47-Year Manhunt." *NPR.com*. NPR, 21 Sep 2009. Web. 17 May 2011.

3. Jolene Babyak. *Breaking The Rock*. Berkeley, CA: Ariel Vamp Press, 2001. Print. 219.

4. Ibid. 225.

5. Ibid. 232.

Chapter 10. Did They Make It?

1. "John Anglin, Clarence Anglin and Frank Lee Morris Escape from Alcatraz." *FBI*. FBI, n.d. File number 76-26295. Volume number 1. Web. 23 May 2011.

2. Jolene Babyak. *Breaking The Rock*. Berkeley, CA: Ariel Vamp Press, 2001. Print. 231.

3. "John Anglin, Clarence Anglin and Frank Lee Morris Escape from Alcatraz." *FBI*. FBI, n.d. File number 76-26295. Volume number 6. Web. 23 May 2011.

4. Phil Long. "Escape from Alcatraz/Ex-convict's new clues renew jail-break tale." *Houston Chronicle*. HoustonChronicle.com, 5 Dec. 1993. Web. 17 May 2011.

5. "John Anglin, Clarence Anglin and Frank Lee Morris Escape from Alcatraz." *FBI*. FBI, n.d. File number 76-26295. Volume number 2. Web. 23 May 2011.

6. "Escape From Alcatraz and a 47-Year Manhunt." *NPR.com*. NPR, 21 Sep 2009. Web. 17 May 2011.

7. Laura Sullivan. "Mystery Still Swirls Around Alcatraz Escape." *90.9 WBUR*. National Public Radio, 22 Sept. 2009. Web. 1 Sept. 2011.

Index

About the Author

Stephanie Watson is a freelance writer based in Atlanta, Georgia. Over her 20-plus-year career, she has written for television, radio, the Web, and print. Stephanie has authored more than two dozen books, including *Messages from Beyond* (fiction), *The United States: Past and Present—Georgia*, *Celebrity Biographies: Daniel Radcliffe*, and *Weird, Wacky and Wild Georgia Trivia* (co-author).

About the Content Consultant

Michael Esslinger is a historical researcher and bestselling author whose acclaimed work has appeared in numerous books and documentaries, including segments on the Discovery, National Geographic, and History Channels. He is considered one of the foremost authorities on the history of Alcatraz.

Photo Credits

Courtesy National Park Service, Museum Management Program and Alcatraz Island/Golden Gate National Recreation Area, www.cr.nps.gov/museum: GOGA 2042, Military Officer at Canon Placement, Fort Alcatraz, 14, 98 (top); GOGA 19200e, Tailor Shop, 29; GOGA 18352d, Correctional Officer Operating the Cell-locking Device, 34; GOGA 18352e, Correctional Officer in Guard Tower, 35; GOGA 96, Tear Gas Canister, Metal, paint, 37; GOGA 2316d, Theodore Cole, 40; GOGA 18261p, James "Tex" Lucas and Rufus "Whitey" Franklin, 43, 99 (top); GOGA 18261h, Arthur "Doc" Barker in County Jail, 44; GOGA 375, Wrench, Metal, plywood, 60; GOGA 362, GOGA 363, and GOGA 364, Bottles, Glass, metal, paint, paper, 63, 97 (bottom); GOGA 356, Ventilator Grille and Board Remnant, Canvas board, soap, paint, metal, 64, 96 (top); GOGA 405, Fake Head, Cotton, soap, paint, human hair, 66, 96 (bottom); GOGA 350, Magazine, Paper, ink, 68; GOGA 372, Drill, Metal, plastic, tape, 71, 97 (top); GOGA 408 and GOGA 409, Paddles, Wood, metal and Wood, metal, paint, 75, 100 (bottom); GOGA 411, Raft, Rubberized fabric, wood, glue, paper, 77; GOGA 18324c, John Anglin Wanted Poster, 83, 101 (bottom)

Alvaro Leiva/Photolibrary, cover, 3; Crossroads Creative/iStockphoto, 7; Historic American Buildings Survey/Library of Congress, 10, 21, 39; AP Images, 17, 19, 26, 89, 98 (bottom); Justin Horrocks/iStockphoto, 22, 105; Daniel Cardiff/iStockphoto, 32; Michael Esslinger, 51, 53, 55, 56, 81, 85, 100 (top); Alcatraz Federal Penitentiary/AP Images, 73; Nat Farbman/Time & Life Pictures/Getty Images, 79, 101 (top); Eric Risberg/AP Images, 93; JTB Photo/Photolibrary, 95